Cat's Cradl

& The World's Best String Games

Günter Frorath

Illustrations by **Marlit Peikert**

 Mud Puddle Books
NEW YORK

Cat's Cradle & The World's Best String Games

Written by Günter Frorath / Illustrations by Marlit Peikert

First published in Germany by moses. Verlag GmbH, Kempen 2002
Text and illustrations © moses. Verlag GmbH, Kempen 2002

Translation © 2005 by Mud Puddle Books, Inc.

English language edition published by
Mud Puddle Books, Inc.
54 W. 21st Street
Suite 601
New York, NY 10010

info@mudpuddlebooks.com

ISBN: 1-59412-093-5

English translation by Katja Yeats

Printed and bound in China

Contents

Hi!

A note from the author

People often ask me: "Who actually invented string games?" And I always reply: "Nobody. And everybody!" Yes, it's really that strange with string games. Their history is definitely shrouded in mystery. They are played all over the world, from Greenland in the far North all the way South to New Zealand. Here's what's even more curious: in regions of the world separated by long distances, people have been weaving the same patterns and figures on their hands for ages. For example, let's take the string game called The Mouse is Gone (you'll find it on page 37 of this book). Eskimos,

Japanese and Australians alike have been playing this game in exactly the same way even though Greenland, Japan and Australia are separated by many thousands of miles of sea. How did string games travel around the world long before there were books like this to explain them? Who invented them? We can speculate and create a plausible scenario something like this: For thousands of years people around the world preferred to play in their spare time rather than be bored. Catching sight of a piece of string, rope, thread or cord while sitting around by themselves or with others, they put it around their fingers and watched what happened. Over time, I think, many similar or even the same string games developed in the igloos of the North Pole and in the tents of the desert. You will find some of the world's best string games in this book. They come from many different regions or our world. Some will be completely new to you, others you may know from friends or your parents. Some are very easy and others will take some practice. But all of them are exciting and fun. And don't worry: every step will be well explained!
So – have fun playing!

Günter Frorath

Near, Far, Right and Left

A few important terms

Learning to play string games is a cinch: a friend shows you or you show a friend. One demonstrates while one watches. It's quick and easy.

It's a little different when string games are explained in a book. The individual steps have to be explained in pictures and words. To begin with and to avoid misunderstandings and complications, it's best to be familiar with a few terms.

This is the string. It can also be called a cord or thread.

If you put the cord around a finger, such as the index finger (like here), you get a loop. You can also call it a noose. Since this loop goes around the index finger it is called the index loop.

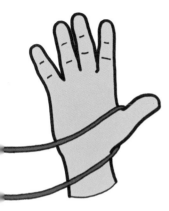

A loop that goes around the thumb is called a thumb loop, and the loop going around the little finger is the little finger loop. And so on and so forth...

Sometimes there are two loops on one finger at the same time. In this case, the loop closest to the fingertip is called the upper loop; the other one is called the lower loop. It doesn't matter if the finger-tips point to the sky or to the floor: up is where the fingernails are!

When you play, your hands move a lot which sometimes makes it difficult to know what's meant by near and far. For the expe-rienced string game player this is no prob-lem at all: simply hold both hands in front of your nose, about a foot away, finger tips up and palms slightly turned toward your face. Put the string around your thumbs. The part of the string that is now in front of your right thumb is called the near right thumb string. The string running behind your left thumb is called the far left thumb string. This is true for all the other fingers.

So: the part of the string closest to your arm is the near string, the other (the part farther away) is the far string. Take a good long look at the drawing:

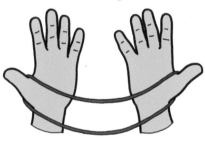

A few tips:
This book comes with a nice long string. But, if you ever lose it, you can make your own string. Take a piece of string, about 6 feet (2 m) long and tie the ends in a knot. The easiest knot to tie is the square knot (also called a reef knot, Hercules knot or weaver's knot). Don't forget that by cutting off the ends very close to the knot, the string will slide better when you're playing.

With the help of an adult you can make a circular (endless) string for string games. You'll need nylon string, which is available in many stores, and a burning candle (that's where the adult help comes in). Ask the adult to heat up the ends of the nylon string over the flame.

The ends will melt. If the adult quickly holds the ends together they will stick together, and you will have a circular (endless) string.

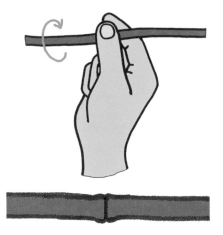

Opening "A"

1 Many string games start this way. This type of opening is called Opening "A." First, put your hands in the basic position. Your palms and fingers are facing each other.

2 Hang the circular string on your thumbs like this:

3 Pick up the back string with your little fingers so that it runs around the little fingers. Isn't that easy?

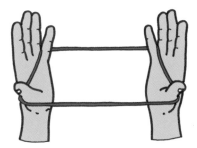

4 Using your right index finger, reach down and pick up the string that runs across your left palm. Do the same with your left index finger, this time picking up the string going across the right palm. Return your hands to the basic position.

5

6

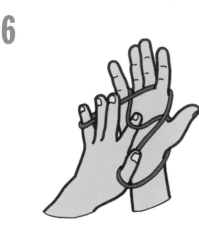

7

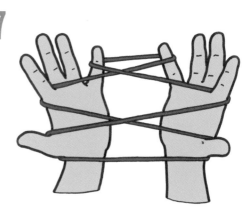

Because this opening is used a lot, it wouldn't be a bad idea to practice it a few times. This way, you definitely won't forget it for the rest of your life!

The Navajo Hop

A super special trick

The name "Navajo Hop" (also called Navajo Jump or Navajo Method) originally came from the Navajo Indians from whom every string game player can learn a lot. For example, you can learn what to do when you have two strings on one finger or thumb and the lower string needs to be lifted up over the upper string without creating a big string mess.

1 So, let's assume the string is on your fingers as shown in this drawing:

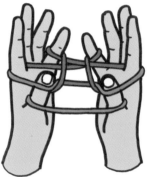

2 Now, you want to lift the lower loop over the upper one. To do this, carefully – like a Navajo – put together your right index finger and thumb. Then, even more carefully, lift up the lower thumb string over the

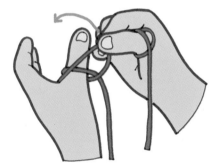

upper one and let it slip off. Your left index finger and thumb will do the same thing to the lower right thumb string. Make sure the upper string doesn't slip off, too!

Another way to make the Navajo Hop – something like the Navajo Chief method – goes like this: don't use your fingers but use your teeth. It's faster, easier and more fun!

However, until you are as good as the escape artist Harry Houdini, you might have to practice a few times.

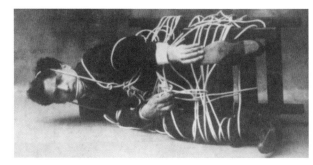

Spectacles

1 You already know the first step because you practiced it earlier: Opening "A."

2 Your thumbs drop their loops.

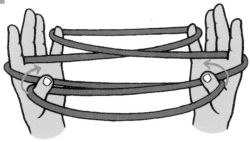

3 Your thumbs move past the strings of the index loops and grasp the near little finger strings. Then your thumbs return.

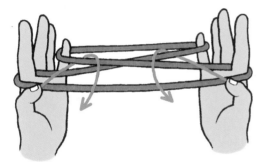

4 Your little fingers drop their loops.

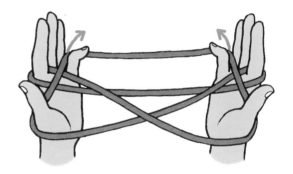

Your thumbs move up into the index loops and return with the near index strings.

Use your teeth or fingers to switch the thumb loops (Navajo Method!).

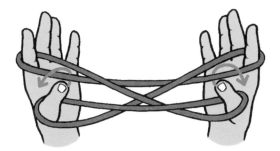

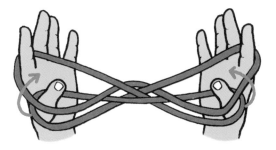

7 Bend your index fingers over the switched loops that now cross in the center of the figure. Continue all the way down into the index loops.

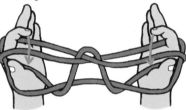

8

9 Turn your hands so that the backs of your hands face you. Straighten your index fingers and look through your new spectacles. Don't worry about the index loops: they will slip off by themselves. Don't pull the figure too tight. Make it tall rather than wide as you extend it.

The Winking Eye

1 Hang the string loop over the fingers of your left hand leaving the thumb free.

2 Close your left middle, ring and little fingers on the string hanging across the palm of your hand. Your index finger is still straight.

3 Your right index finger and thumb take the back string of the hanging loop. Wrap it all the way around your left index finger and hang it up on your thumb.

4 Your right index finger and thumb extend the loop hanging on your left index finger and pull it over the left thumb. Your left index finger and left thumb are sharing the loop. Make sure you don't twist the loop when you do this.

5 Take the string of the hanging loop nearest to you and lift it up over the string running between index finger and thumb. Let it hang down in front of the string between the index finger and thumb.

6 Take the other string of the hanging loop (the loop you just held) and lift it up so that it hangs over your thumb.

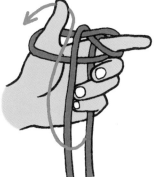

7 To make the eye wink, pull the strings of the hanging loop sideways. Then let your left index finger and thumb come closer together.

8 To open the eye, pull your left index finger and thumb farther apart. Then loosen your hold on the hanging loop, and the eye will wink at you ☺.

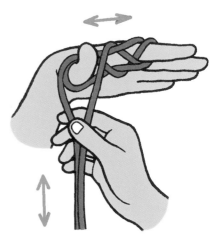

A String Trick

1 Put the string loop around your neck below your ears and level with your mouth. Hold the side strings fairly high so that you can cross them over easily.

2 Cross the strings over each other and hold them with your teeth where they cross. Cross your arms as you do this. Don't change hands and don't let go of the strings.

3 Now uncross your arms. At the same time, the strings will uncross in your mouth. Nobody will see this as the strings are hidden behind your lips.

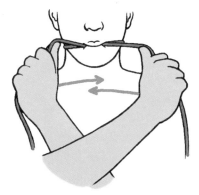

4 Pull the long string loop over your head. Your hands are still holding the ends of the loop.

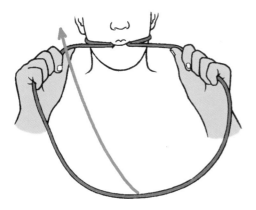

5 Now clap your hands (while still holding the strings).

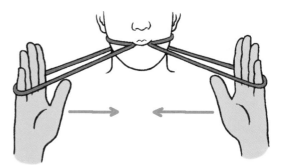

6 Let go of the strings in your mouth and stretch out your arms. Now, everybody will see that the string loop is behind the back of your neck and will be amazed at how you magically uncrossed the strings!

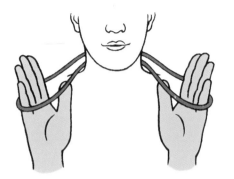

This trick is from the Bantu people of Africa. It's not difficult, but it never fails to amaze people, especially if it's done quickly. Don't forget to clap your hands. It makes this trick more exciting!

Cup and Saucer

1 Start this string game with Opening "A."

2 After the opening you will do something completely new. Move your thumbs to the string running behind the index fingers and pull them up behind the string and back towards you. Now, each thumb has not one but two loops. This makes the heart of the Navajo skip a beat! Now the lower loop will have to be lifted over the upper loop. High time for the Navajo Hop!

31

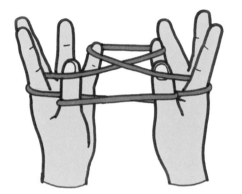

3 Using your teeth, carefully pick up the lower thumb string, lift it up over the upper string (the string that was your lower string just a second ago) and let it slip off behind your thumb. Make sure that the upper string doesn't slip off, too!

The figure on your hands should look like this:

4 From now on it's really easy. Drop the loops on your little fingers or, better yet, carefully let them slip off.

5

6 Now you have a large loop in the back. Not for long though. Pull your hands apart vertically and stretch your fingers so that the string figure is very tight.

7 Rotate the whole figure so that the tips of your thumbs point away from you. Now you can see it: a large cup with a saucer.

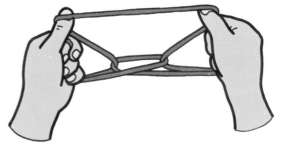

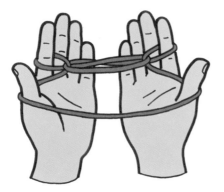

Eiffel Tower

Start with the cup and saucer. Point the saucer away from you and the top of the cup toward you as it is lying between your thumbs. Hold the string with your teeth. Take out your thumbs leaving the figure held by your teeth and your index fingers. Gently move your hands down along your body. Voila! You're in Paris!

Clothes Hanger

Now that you're in Paris, you might as well stay a few days because it's so nice. But unfortunately ...there are no hangers in your hotel room. But this isn't a problem for you at all. You'll just make a hanger out of the Eiffel Tower!

Like this:

Slowly and carefully pull your index fingers apart. This will just as slowly and carefully move the knot in the middle of the figure to the top. Once it is fairly close to your mouth the clothes hanger is done.

Now you can hang your coat on it and enjoy a cup of cocoa. Of course, this cup is standing on a large saucer. And you know how to make a cup and saucer...

The Mouse Is Gone

1

Before the mouse can disappear in the end, you have to create it on your hand.

Like this:

Hold your left hand in front of your body. Your palm faces you, thumb is up and your remaining fingers are straight and point to the right. Lay a piece of string over the thumb: one part hangs down in front of your hand, the other part hangs behind your hand.

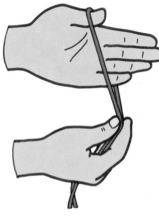

2 Move your right index finger underneath the near left thumb string and pull it over the string between thumb and index finger. The arrow will show you the way.

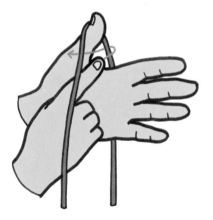

3 Move your right index finger over the string. Then grab it with your curled fingertip and pull forward.

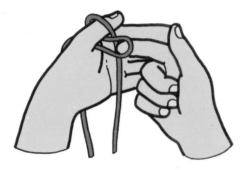

4 Rotate your right index finger and the loop half a turn clockwise.

Hang the loop on your left index finger.

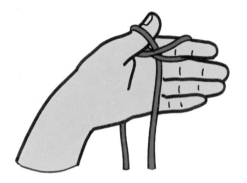

6

Tighten the loop by pulling on the strings that are hanging down. Here we go! As before, move the right index finger underneath the string in front of you, but this time move the right index finger between your left index and middle finger. From above, grab the string behind the left index finger and pull it forward. Again, rotate your right index finger and the loop half a turn clockwise and hang the loop on the middle finger. Pull!

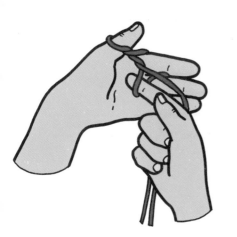

7 Rotate your right index finger and the loop half a turn clockwise and hang the loop on the middle finger. Pull!

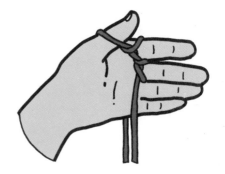

8 Do the same with the ring finger and the little finger. Pull on the hanging ends of string once more so that they run along the bottom of your fingers.

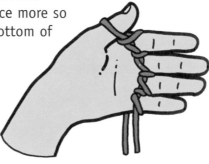

9 Show your audience this magic piece of art. Once everybody is done being amazed, pull the left thumb out of its loop.

Now pull on the string hanging in front – that is, toward your body – and bam! the mouse is gone!

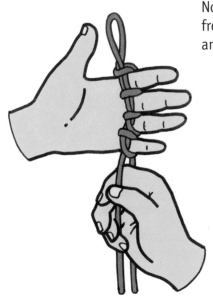

Two Diamonds

1 Begin with Opening "A."

2 Take your thumbs out of the thumb loops. Carefully pull your hands apart.

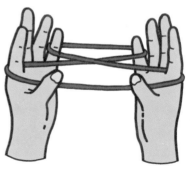

3 Move your thumbs across all of the strings to the farthest string. Hook this string onto your thumbs from below and pull it toward you.

4 The string is now all the way up front. Now, pay attention! Put both thumbs into the index loops. Do it exactly as shown by the arrows.

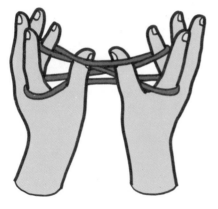

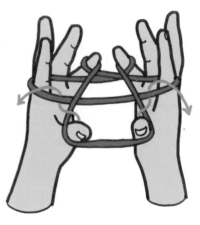

5 Move the first string over and under the second string. Use your other hand to help. Start with the left thumb. It should look like this:

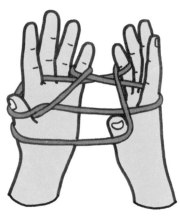

6 Continue with the right thumb. Now you have two loops on each thumb.

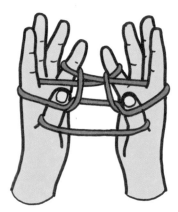

7 Pick up the string between the two thumbs with you teeth and complete the famous Navajo Hop. After that, your string figure should look like this:

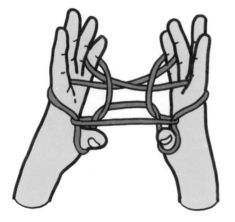

8 Now you have a small triangle in front of each thumb. Take a look at the drawing.

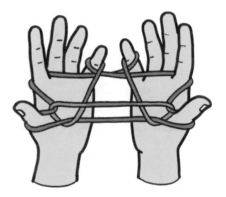

9 Put your index fingers into these triangles from above and tightly press your fingers against the balls of your thumbs.

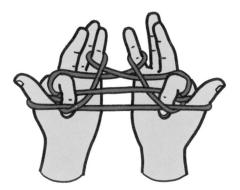

10 Turn your palms downward, the fingertips pointing away from you, and take your little fingers out of the string loops. Use your other hand to help.

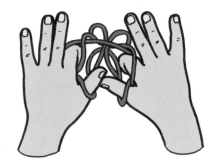

11 Carefully spread apart your thumbs and index fingers. Make sure the strings don't slip off your thumbs! There, two diamonds sparkling in your hands!

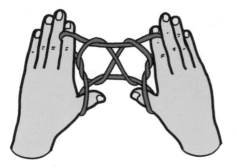

If you double your string for this game, the diamonds will look particularly nice. However, you will have to move your fingers even more carefully.

The Released Hand

1 For this game, you will need a partner. Once again, begin with Opening "A."

2 Let's get started. Ask your partner to put his/her hand from the top into the large plane held by your index fingers on the left and right side.

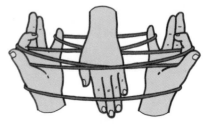

3 Let the loops on your index and little fingers slip off. The string will tighten when your thumbs pull out their loops. Suddenly, your friend's hand is trapped in a tight loop!

4 Now, your little fingers pick up the two strings running behind your thumbs toward the trapped hand.

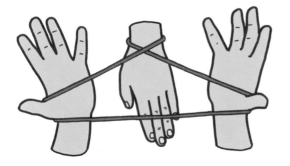

5 Go back to the basic position used in the beginning of this game. Your right index finger goes underneath the palm string of your left hand and your left index finger goes underneath the palm string of your right hand.

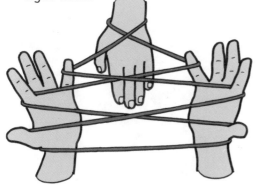

6 Again, you're holding a figure with lots of planes. Ask your partner to put his hand through the center plane (like before), but this time from the bottom to the top.

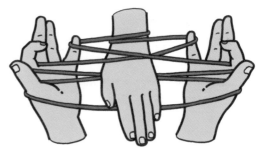

7 Will he ever be released from these gripping strings? We'll see! Your index and little fingers drop their loops. Now you have a mess of string! Not for long though. Your thumbs simply pull apart their loops. The whole mess of string disappears into thin air, and the hand is released!

The Fly

1 Start out by putting the string loop around your little fingers.

Move your thumbs behind both strings.

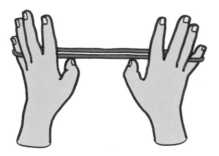

Now the string figure looks like the one in the following drawing.

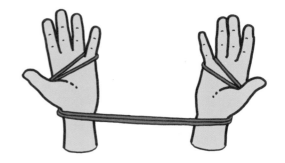

4 From below, your right index finger gets the strings running in front of your left palm.

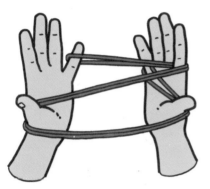

5 Your left thumb moves past the strings between your hands and picks up from below the two strings in front of your right little finger. Your figure now looks like this:

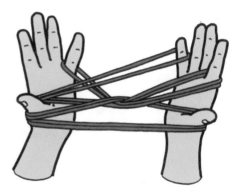

6 Your left thumb now holds two loops. Time to do a Navajo Hop! So, grasp the two lower left thumb strings with your teeth and pull them over the two upper strings. Make sure they don't slip off your thumb, too!

7 Now, the string figure looks pretty complicated. But it will soon become easier again. Pull the right thumb out of its loop. You now have a nice knot between your hands. Now, pull your left thumb out of its loop, then the right index finger.

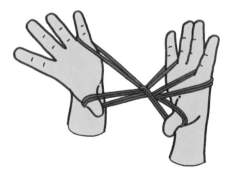

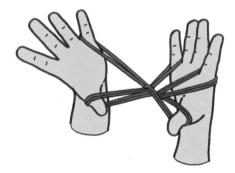

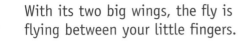

8 With its two big wings, the fly is flying between your little fingers.

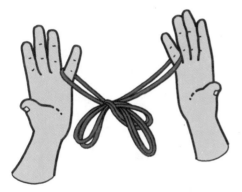

The World Famous Game of Cat's Cradle

If you're by yourself and don't know what to play you can pass time quite well by making string figures. But it's even nicer if two can play. That's why so many kids around the world like to play Cat's Cradle for four hands. If there are other kids standing around in a circle, amazed at all the transformations happening on your hands, don't be surprised when they say, "I want to learn that, too!" This makes the game is even better!

The string figures created during a game of Cat's Cradle are called different names. What we call "The Mirror" is also known as "The Calm Sea." The main point is: playing Cat's Cradle is fun!

By the way, when playing Cat's Cradle, the players shouldn't sit opposite or next to each other. The best position for playing Cat's Cradle is when the players sit at a slight angle to each other.

We have marked the two players with A and B so that you can easily follow which hands belong to which player. Let's get started!

From the Basic Position to the Mattress

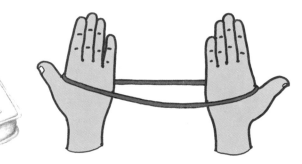

1 A begins and puts the string over the back of each hand. The thumbs remain outside of the string.

2 A puts his/her right hand under the front string of the left hand and pulls his/her hands apart. The same is done with the left hand.

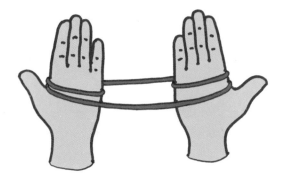

3 The right index finger goes under the string in front of the left palm. Then, the same is done in reverse, like this: the left index finger goes under the string in front of the right palm. A pulls the figure apart. A is now done with the basic position. It should look like this...

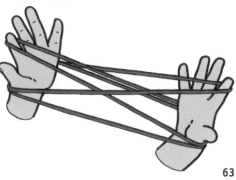

4 ...and B can start something new with it. Let's go! From the outside, B firmly grasps the two upper crosses of the figure with the thumb and index finger of both hands.

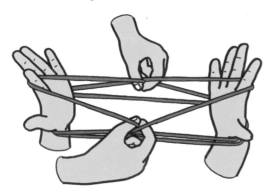

5 B pulls both hands out to the sides over the two lower strings. His/her hands come back up in the center of the string rectangle.

6 A removes his/her fingers and the figure is now held by B. B spreads index fingers and thumbs and pulls his/her hands apart. The mattress!

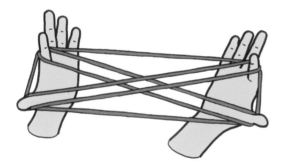

From the Mattress to the Mirror

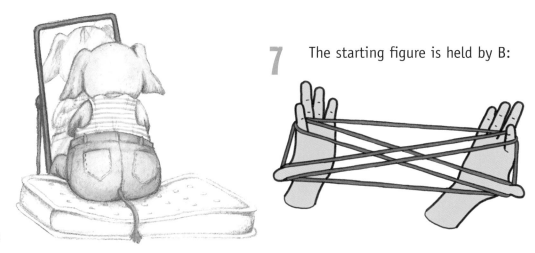

7 The starting figure is held by B:

8 From above, A grasps the crosses closest to the outside strings using his/her thumbs and index fingers.

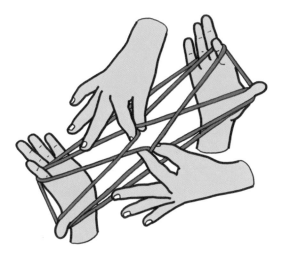

9 A now pulls both hands out to the sides over the side strings and comes back up in the middle of the string rectangle. B removes his/her hands.

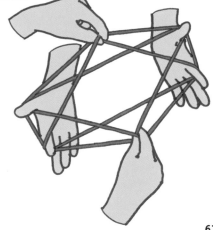

10 And now we have a nice, rectangular mirror.

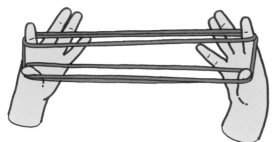

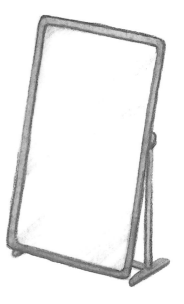

From the Mirror to the Cradle

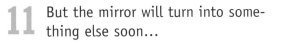

11 But the mirror will turn into something else soon...

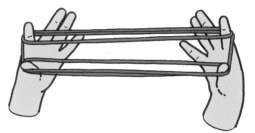

12 Holding the right little finger like a hook, B grasps from below the string running on the inside left of the figure from his/her point of view and pulls it out over the right outside string. The same is done with the left hand, but, of course, in the mirror image.

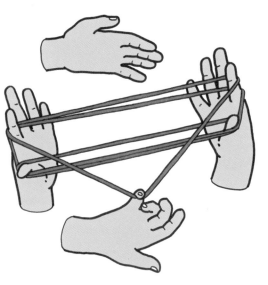

13 B now moves his/her thumbs and index fingers from above into the newly formed outside triangles.

Thumbs and index fingers come back up in the middle of the figure.

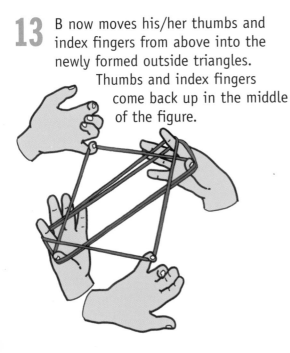

14 A takes his/her fingers out of the figure. B spreads thumbs and index fingers and pulls his/her hands apart.

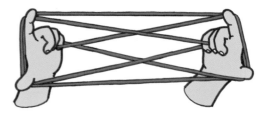

From the Cradle to the Diamond

15 The cradle won't be a cradle for long...

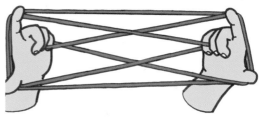

16 Using thumbs and index fingers, A grasps the crosses from the outside as shown in the drawing.

17 A pulls the crosses out past the outside strings and into the figure from above.

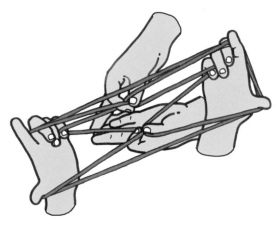

18 B removes his/her hands. A spreads thumbs and index fingers and pulls his/her hands apart. And now you see a beautiful diamond sparkle!

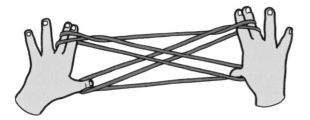

From the Diamond to the Cat's Eye

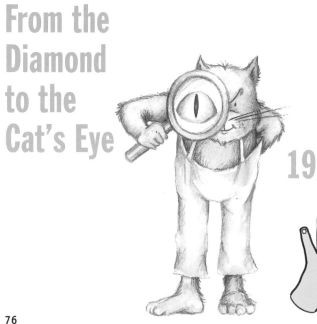

19 But soon something different will look out of your figure...

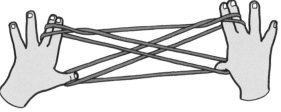

20 From above, B first grasps the crosses that are closest to the outside strings using thumbs and index fingers. Then B pulls the crosses out past the long strings and comes back up in the middle of the figure.

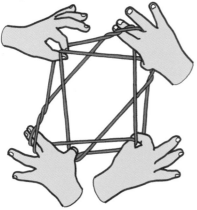

21 A removes his/her hands. B spreads thumbs and index fingers and pulls both hands apart, and suddenly, a cat's eye stares at you!

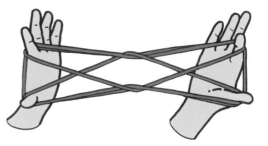

From the Cat's Eye to the Sleeping Bear

22 Pretty soon, the eye will get tired...

23 Using the thumbs and index fingers, A grasps from above the crosses on the edge of the figure.

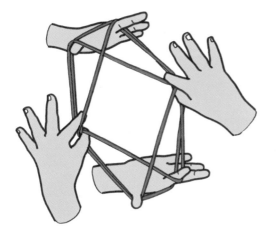

24 A rotates his/her thumbs and index fingers upward. B removes his/her hands. A spreads thumbs and index fingers and pulls his/her hands apart.

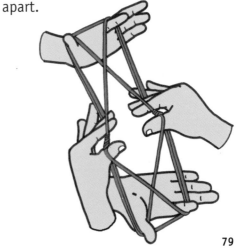

25 There is the bear – sleeping and completely stretched out!